Strange Girl

Alanna Higginson

Presentation by *BookLeaf Publishing*

Web: www.bookleafpub.com

E-mail: info@bookleafpub.com

ISBN: 9789357696548

First edition 2022

Lemon Sherbet

Tasty, lemon sherbet
hard on the outside
but
like some people
deliciously sweet
with a touch of bitterness
inside.

Labels Are For Jam

Are you gay, straight,
Femme, butch,
Fat or thin?
Why are we so preoccupied with labels
Trying to fit in
Does it matter what clothes I wear?
I am a mum who has never given birth
A sibling to four others
Yet my parents only child.
I am your best friend
Your neighbour
Lover
Sister
All different things at the same time
I am real
So go ahead
Label me!
Who needs to fit inside a box so badly
That we deny ourselves
The other part of who we really are,
Who we can be...
I am so much more than the sum of my parts
All of us are.
Are we parodies of ourselves?
Conflicted
Ironic
Sarcastic
Sometimes downright bloody difficult.

I am a woman who loves women
Yet will never understand the female psyche
Anymore than a man;
Slightly jaded, I remain ever the optimist
We are alike, you and I
Only not the same
I don't like to label what I refuse to define.
The truly amazing
Delightful
Wonderful thing about people
Is their complexity
Changeability
Spontaneity.
You can't put a label on that!

The Dark

The moon casts her light
Into a sky of black ink
Projecting shadows around every corner.
Darkness
Blankets my thoughts and fears,
Quietness engulfs me
Daring me to breathe
As I may be heard,
Night time
Seems like an eternity
Before the refuge of morning begins.

Loneliness

You will have to excuse me if I am rambling,
struggling for words at times
you see, I am grasping at a new language,
the language of loneliness.
Now that I have spoken the word
I see you nervously seeking an exit,
you would sooner I rehearsed my words on
someone else.
But the words are still there
if you choose to hear them or not?
I have been practising for some time now
empowering myself with verse
about anguish,
despair
isolation
and the torture of my mind.
Loneliness is a hidden language,
repressed by those it frightens
but loneliness is stronger and more intense
than any other language I know.

Mum

She has forgotten
the day
the place
the time
but -
she remembers
children
laughter
and love.

Teenage Years

My teens spent listening
to the Same Sky with my girlfriends
I never imagined that I would
Make sweet music with you.
You, who inspires me every single day
You, who looks beyond the chaos of my mind
You, who truly believes in me
Us.
You are the wind beneath my wings
Encouraging me to fly.

It's Hard Just to Be

It's hard to be anxious when you have a loving family
and truly loyal friends.
It's difficult to accept that you are feeling down
have your son's arm wrapped around you,
new work opportunities presented, and your friends
are behaving ridiculously just to make you laugh.
It's a struggle to realise you are wading like a duck
through water,
Gliding on the surface, but paddling furiously
underneath,
But I am.
Some days are better than others.
Standing in front of my parents I smile
Laugh at dad's jokes, his funny ways
It isn't forced, I want you to understand that.
It's hard struggling to breathe through panic attacks
while life continues
The world still spins with me on the treadmill of life.
Everyday a gamble, life like a deck of cards
Never knowing which hand you will be dealt.
Life isn't always like this.
Sometimes, it's hard just to be...

Spirit

If my spirit is an ocean
Then I am caught
In the unfathomable depths,
White foam suds
Suffocating my soul.

Strange Girl

They said I was a strange girl
I had no idea
They said I was a fat girl,
Ugly, queer
Those were the words I began to hear.
Barbed, piercing words - stabbing
Slicing at me
Hurting.
They stripped my identity
Peeling me
Layer by layer
Until I found myself drowning
In a sea of self doubt
And you?
Having a laugh, poking fun
Faceless keyboard warriors all,
Cowardice coated in bravery
Locked and loaded, astride your tanks
Blithely firing your hate.
Tomorrow, because of you
I could be dead
Today,
This strange girl is very much alive.

Torn

Darkness blankets my room
Where on the bed
I lie silently between two lovers,
Life and Death.
Enveloped by a sheet of pain
No longer the light of my dreams before me
I ask each one 'who are you?'
The answer is simple
I am a saint, I am a sinner
Not worthy of living , too young for hell,
A moment suspended in time
Until my clock stopped ticking
For a morning that never came.

Masterpiece

My canvas is a sheet of pale flesh
Blades are my brushes
Blood is my paint,
I dabble in different shades of crimson
Artist of my own destruction
Pictures tell a story of my past,
What is yet to come.
In this chaotic beauty lie wounded works of art
Vividly remembering the day
My son stared at my masterpiece
Mixed with pity and disgust
I flushed with shame,
Letting go of my tears
Laid down my steely brush and
From that moment
I never painted again.

Scorpion

Indignant I rise
Grasping pincers
Warning.
Venom
Poised to strike
You powerless
A mother will always protect her young
Beware the sting in my tail.

The Girl I Used to Be

Brief glimpses of those colourful days
Once bright eyes, a future unplanned
Now hauntingly on my muddled mind play
Life is written in the sand.

Surrounded by people, yet all alone
Voices interrupt, begging to be heard
Throughout childhood the seeds were sown
Telling me 'I am not worthy, I do not deserve'.

Trapped inside this self-imposed prison
Riddled with conflict and despair
At the mercy of constant derision
Poisoning my mind, too much to bear.

When merely existing has no meaning or hope
On this strange planet called insanity
Truth hangs on by a withered rope
All senses heightened by anxiety.

Into adulthood the die was cast
By demons only I can see
Among cluttered archives of the past
Lie the memories of, the girl I used to be.

Under a Melbourne Sky

That carefree summer afternoon
Our lips barely left each other
Kissing under a Melbourne sky
Heavy clouds interrupt
Cool air meets skin on fire,
Dark skies revealed inseparable lovers
Time stopped still for a moment
Lightning flashed, twisted and white
For us alone the universe came alive
We yelled promises between thunderbolts
To grow old together
Then silently, we ran towards our future
Laughing.

Menopausal Seasons

Women, like a dense forest
Full of colour and delight one season,
Stripped bare, dejected the next.
In a good mood, full of vibrancy and life
From Autumn to Winter
Embittered, frozen
switched off –
They haven't even a leaf to offer you...
As the wind changes direction
Seasons come and go
So do the mood swings
Swaying
Like the bough of a tree.

Chameleon

I see a stranger in her eyes
Where I once found my soulmate
Her magical kiss
Now frozen in to oblivion.
Her face is unreadable, heart always changing
To no one has she ever shown her true colours,
A shade of red showing danger
Green, jealousy opening the floodgates of destruction
Distant eyes, ice-cold blue, are revealed.
Powerfully, she knows how to promise and deceive
Her smile victorious.

Me, Myself and I

Stop trying so hard, little one
Stop following the crowd
Stop working so hard to make people like you
Stop being someone you were never meant to be
Stop crying tears over someone that doesn't want you
Stop worrying so much about what everyone else
thinks
Stop fading into the background
Stop being afraid to stand out.

Live your life authentically
Know your truth
Stand by the ones that love you
Create you own happiness
Know you are worthy.

Stranded

She disappeared in the dead of winter
Towards the shallow depths of deceit
Me, rudderless in a sea of confusion.
Waves lap against my eyelids
Where a million broken dreams swim
Out of reach.
Love is lost in the ocean that divides us
Gulls swoop, faithless
Leaving only bitter regret.

Marilyn

There is a moment
In some womens' lives
When they put on bright red lipstick
For the very first time
Stride out into the world
Feeling more beautiful and alive
Than they ever have, ever will again
And somewhere up above
I like to imagine
Marilyn Monroe is smiling.

Unmarried

I am in our home
You are everywhere
But not here
Grey walking jacket hanging in the hallway
Transparent window panes frosted
With the cool heat of disinterest.
Tonight, I opened a book from the bedside table
Found a flower you'd pressed,
It was tiny
In greens and yellows, defining a love now dead
Sheets once weighted with passion
Now a heavy burden in a darkening room.
I sleep in the middle of the bed
Learn how to fill the coffee pot for one,
For all the things I'd hoped we would be
I never once imagined 'strangers',
It's been the hardest goodbye -
Pretending to unlove you every day.